DAYS THAT SHOOK THE WORLD

ASSASSINATION IN SARAJEVO

28 JUNE 1914

Alex Woolf

an imprint of Hodder Children's Books

DAYS THAT SHOOK THE WORLD

Produced by Monkey Puzzle Media Ltd
Gissing's Farm, Fressingfield
Suffolk IP21 5SH

First published in 2002 by Hodder Wayland
An imprint of Hodder Children's Books
Text copyright © 2002 Hodder Wayland
Volume copyright © 2002 Hodder Wayland

Series Concept: Liz Gogerly
Editor: Jason Hook
Design: Jane Hawkins
Picture Researcher: Lynda Lines
Consultant: Michael Rawcliffe

Cover picture: Moments after the shooting of Archduke Franz Ferdinand,
the assassin Gavrilo Princip is arrested.
Title page picture: The archduke and his wife (in the back of the car) on
what was to be their last journey.

We are grateful to the following for permission to reproduce photographs:
AKG 2, 6, 9 bottom (Alte Nationalgalerie), 10 11 top, 18, 19, 21 top, 24 top (Erich Lessing), 29, 30, 31 top, 38, 39, 40; Corbis front cover (Bettmann), 20 (Bettmann), 22 left (Otto Lang), 23 (Bettmann), 25 (Bettmann), 26 (Bettmann), 28 (Bettmann), 32 (Hulton-Deutsch Collection), 41 (Michael S Yamashita), 46 (Michael S Yamashita); Hulton Archive 17, 22 right, 31 bottom, 34; Mary Evans Picture Library 12, 16, 24 bottom; Popperfoto 11 bottom, 13, 27, 35 bottom, 36, 37, 42, 43; Topham Picturepoint 7, 8, 14 left, 14 right, 15. Artwork on pages 9, 21, 33 and 35 by Michael Posen.

Printed and bound in Italy by G. Canale & C.Sp.A, Turin

British Library Cataloguing in Publication Data
Woolf, Alex
Assassination in Sarajevo. - (Days that shook the world)
1.Franz Ferdinand, Archduke of Austria, 1863-1914 - Assassination
2.World War, 1914-1918 - Causes - Juvenile literature
I.Title
940.5'3112

ISBN 07502 3569 1
Hodder Children's Books
A division of Hodder Headline Limited
338 Euston Road, London NW1 3BH

CONTENTS

Archduke Franz Ferdinand (left) and his wife, Sophie, arrive in Sarajevo on the morning of 28 June 1914.

ARCHDUKE FRANZ FERDINAND, HEIR to the throne of the Austro-Hungarian Empire, was in a contented mood. Accompanied by his dear wife Sophie, he was on an official visit to Bosnia, a southern province of the empire. The archduke enjoyed getting away from Vienna, the capital of Austria-Hungary, where he was out of favour with his uncle, the emperor Franz Joseph.

Franz Ferdinand was inspector general of the empire's armed forces. He had been invited by Bosnia's governor, General Oskar Potiorek, to inspect units of the imperial army stationed near the province's capital city of Sarajevo. The archduke and Sophie had spent an enjoyable two days in the mountains above the city watching the troops carry out manoeuvres. Now, on the morning of the final day of their visit, the royal couple were to attend an official reception at City Hall hosted by the mayor of Sarajevo.

Franz Ferdinand had married Sophie Chotek, Duchess of Hohenberg, fourteen years before, almost to the day. Although she had a title, Sophie was not of royal blood and had never really been accepted by the royal family. She was not even allowed to ride in the same car as her husband on official occasions in Vienna. But this rule did not apply in provincial cities like Sarajevo. One of the reasons why Franz Ferdinand had accepted this invitation was to give his wife the opportunity to sit next to him in an open car on a state visit. This was to be his special gift to her, to celebrate their wedding anniversary.

But not everyone in Sarajevo was pleased to see the archduke. Bosnia had been ruled by the Austro-Hungarian Empire since 1878, and in 1908 had formally become part of the empire. In Bosnia, this angered a large minority of people who came originally from the neighbouring country of Serbia.

A Moment in Time

Among the crowd lining Appel Quay, the wide riverside avenue where today's royal procession will take place, are seven young Bosnian Serbs. They are unsmiling and alert. One of them, Danilo Ilic, paces the route. He checks that his comrades are in position, and offers them some words of encouragement. Another, a pale and sickly young man with a thin moustache, stands near the Lateiner Bridge. His name is Gavrilo Princip, and he has a gun hidden in his pocket. These men have prepared a very special welcome for the archduke.

These Bosnian Serbs hated being ruled by Austria-Hungary, and dreamed of the day when Bosnia would become part of a Greater Serbia.

The Serbs were particularly angered by the timing of the archduke's visit, because 28 June was a day of great significance in the Serbian calendar. It was Vid's Day, on which they celebrated both Vid – the Slavic god of war and symbol of Serbia – and the anniversary of Serbia's heroic defeat by the Turks in 1389 at the Battle of Kosovo.

It had been four years since a senior member of the royal family had been to Sarajevo, and some of the archduke's ministers had warned him against the visit. But Franz Ferdinand had dismissed their fears, and he refused to let such thoughts disturb his happy mood.

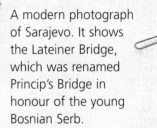

A modern photograph of Sarajevo. It shows the Lateiner Bridge, which was renamed Princip's Bridge in honour of the young Bosnian Serb.

AUSTRIA-HUNGARY, THE EMPIRE to which Franz Ferdinand was heir, was one of the five Great Powers that dominated Europe in 1914. The others were Germany, Britain, France and Russia. For decades, the strength of all these countries had been growing.

Each of the Great Powers had developed both a sense of its own greatness, and a desire to increase its power and influence. Over the previous forty years, each had spent enormous sums of money on building up its army and navy in an attempt to gain an advantage over its rivals.

A major source of tension at this time lay in the south-east of Europe, in a region called the Balkans. This region contained Bosnia, the province where the archduke was making his visit. For many hundreds of years, the Balkans had been controlled by the Turks, and formed the north-western tip of the Turks' enormous Ottoman Empire. But the Ottoman Empire was now in decline. All the Great Powers were interested in one question – who would gain control of the Balkans when the crumbling Ottoman Empire finally collapsed?

BALKAN TROUBLES

This cartoon from the early 1900s shows the leaders of Europe's Great Powers (left to right, Russia, Britain, Germany, France and Austria-Hungary) trying to keep the unrest in the Balkans from 'boiling over'.

The Dual Monarchy

The empire of Austria, which included the kingdom of Hungary, had been ruled by the Habsburg family since 1804. But by the 1860s, a series of military defeats had weakened Austria, and Hungary demanded to have equal status. This led to the formation in 1867 of Austria-Hungary or the Austro-Hungarian Empire. Austria and Hungary would each have its own government, but foreign and military affairs would be conducted jointly from Vienna. So, outwardly at least, Austria-Hungary became a unified empire. In June 1867, the emperor of Austria, Franz Joseph, was crowned king of the newly established nation of Hungary. From this point, Austria-Hungary was known as the Dual Monarchy.

Russia and Austria-Hungary had particular interests in the Balkans. There was a growing desire among the Slavs – an ethnic group living within the Ottoman Empire in Serbia, Croatia, Slovenia, Macedonia and Bulgaria – to form their own separate nation. This worried the leaders of the Austro-Hungarian Empire, which contained many different ethnic groups. The creation of an independent Slav nation to the south might encourage the Slavs of Austria-Hungary, who made up 46 per cent of the population, to call for independence. In Russia, on the other hand, the majority of people were Slavs and the country's leaders had a lot of sympathy for Slav nationalism. It was also in Russia's interests to encourage any movement that challenged its Austro-Hungarian rival.

In 1878, following a short war between Russia and the Turks, a treaty had been drawn up at the Congress of Berlin. Its terms had established or confirmed the independence of Serbia, Montenegro and Romania from the Ottoman Empire. This was good news for Russia and the Slav peoples. But the bad news for them was that in the same treaty, Austria-Hungary was given control of the regions of Bosnia and Herzegovina.

In this way, Austria-Hungary had achieved its twin goals of maintaining a foothold in the Balkans and keeping Slav nationalism contained. But the tension in the region would continue to grow.

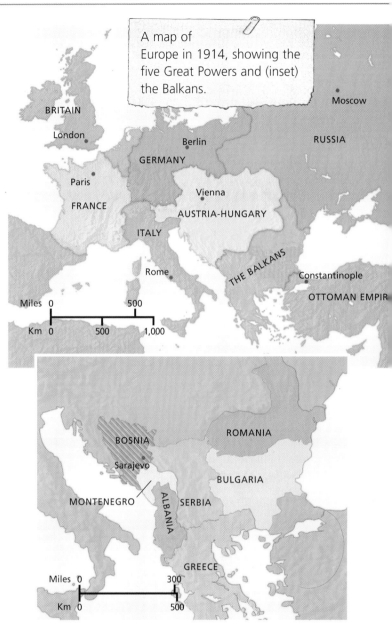

A map of Europe in 1914, showing the five Great Powers and (inset) the Balkans.

A painting of the 1878 Congress of Berlin. This resulted in major political changes for the Balkans. It also led to a greater rivalry between Russia and Austria-Hungary.

By 1914, HISTORIC RIVALRIES between the Great Powers, and the alarming pace at which they were building up their armed forces, were threatening the peace of Europe. These factors alone were unlikely to lead to a general European war. But they were made more perilous by the system of alliances that connected and divided the Great Powers.

The roots of this alliance system lay in the Franco-Prussian War of 1870–71. Germany at this time had been a confederation of thirty-nine separate states, dominated by the kingdom of Prussia. France was defeated in the war, and this led to Prussia forming the German states into a united Germany. The birth of this large nation was disturbing to the other European powers. France, in particular, longed to avenge its defeat and win back the territory it had lost.

The first chancellor of the new Germany, Otto von Bismarck, tried to secure the position of his young nation by using diplomacy to isolate France. He achieved this by making secret military agreements with Austria-Hungary and Russia, creating what was known as the Three Emperors' League. Britain at this time would not be drawn into alliance with anyone, so France was left with no major power to support any bid for revenge against Germany.

However, Russia and Austria-Hungary were not natural allies. Their different ambitions in the Balkans brought them into conflict. Bismarck realized this, and chose to establish closer ties with Austria-Hungary. Germany signed the Dual Alliance with Austria-Hungary in 1879, and this became the Triple Alliance when Italy joined in 1882.

In 1890, Bismarck was dismissed by the new emperor of Germany, Kaiser Wilhelm II, who allowed the secret agreement with Russia to lapse. Russia was now approached by France, and in 1894 the two countries formed the Franco-Russian Alliance. By 1900, Britain was also in search of allies to help keep its empire secure. Kaiser Wilhelm was Queen Victoria's grandson, so Germany seemed the natural choice, but the two

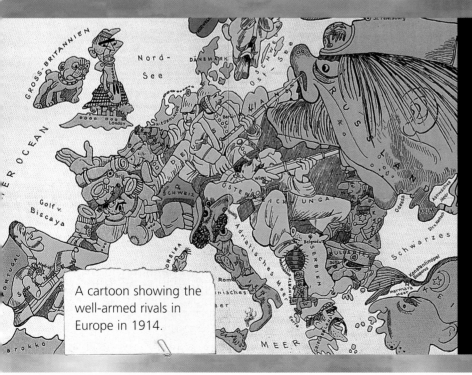

A cartoon showing the well-armed rivals in Europe in 1914.

A Chain Reaction

" If France is attacked by Germany, or by Italy supported by Germany, Russia shall employ all her available forces to attack Germany. If Russia is attacked by Germany, or by Austria supported by Germany, France shall employ all her available forces to fight Germany. "

A secret clause From the Franco-Russian Convention of 1892, which led to the Alliance of 1894.

countries failed to reach any agreement. So, Britain also turned to France. By 1907, France, Russia and Britain were aligned together, forming the Triple Entente.

The major powers of Europe had become divided into two hostile camps: Britain, France and Russia on one side; and Germany, Austria-Hungary and Italy on the other. The most likely flashpoint for a conflict between these two sets of allies was in the Balkans, which both Austria-Hungary and Russia wished to control. The alliance system meant that a local war between these two powers might now set off a chain reaction, leading to a war involving the whole of Europe.

This 1914 French postcard shows the boots of the Triple Entente of (left to right) France, Russia and Britain kicking Kaiser Wilhelm II of Germany.

The meeting in 1872 between Bismarck (centre) and the Russian (left) and Austro-Hungarian foreign ministers, which brought about the Three Emperors' League.

THE ALLIANCE SYSTEM HELD Europe in a very delicate balance, since one small crisis could tip the whole continent into war. In 1908, a crisis in the Balkans nearly did just that.

Small, independent nations, including Serbia, Bulgaria and Albania, had been established in the Balkans as the Ottoman Empire broke up. These small states acted as an inspiration for all minority groups who wished to form their own countries in the Balkans, and their nationalist causes were supported by Russia.

Austria-Hungary opposed these causes, fearing they might lead to pressure for independence from the minority groups within its own empire. Austria-Hungary particularly distrusted Serbia, fearing that it might become the centre of a new Slav state which could pose a threat to Austria-Hungary.

In 1908, the Austrian Foreign Minister, Baron Alois Aehrenthal, decided to provide a demonstration of Austro-Hungarian power in the Balkans by sending in troops to annex – or absorb – the provinces of Bosnia and Herzegovina into the empire. These provinces had been administered by Austria-Hungary since 1878, but were still officially Turkish possessions.

In this 1908 cartoon, the Turkish leader Abdul Hamid II watches helplessly as pieces of the Ottoman Empire are ripped away by Austria-Hungary and Bulgaria.

Kaiser Willhelm II (far right) and Emperor Franz Joseph (centre) in May 1908. Germany would support Austria-Hungary in its stand-off with Russia five months later.

Aehrenthal did not wish to provoke a war with Russia, so he warned the Russian Foreign Minister, Alexander Izvolsky, of his intentions.

When the annexation took place, Serbia was outraged. A large minority of people in Bosnia were of Serb origin, and Serbia had hoped the province would one day be absorbed within Serbia's own borders. Despite the warning received by Izvolsky, Russia felt it had to side with Serbia in the dispute. Relations between Russia and Austria-Hungary became very strained, and there was even talk of war.

Germany came out in support of Austria-Hungary. Helmuth von Moltke, the German Chief of Staff, declared: 'At the same time Russia mobilizes, Germany will mobilize also, and will mobilize her whole army.' The Russians were not strong enough to go to war at this time, having recently been defeated in a conflict with Japan. Neither were Britain or France prepared to support the Russians, so they reluctantly backed down.

The Bosnian Crisis led the Great Powers to rethink their strategies, in ways that actually made conflict more likely the next time there was a crisis. Austria-Hungary became even more distrustful of Serbia and

the Serb nationalists in Bosnia. The strong support offered by Moltke to Austria-Hungary tied Germany even more closely to its aggressive, but weaker, ally. Meanwhile, the Russians decided that 1908 would be the last time they would be humiliated in the Balkans. Next time, they would stand and fight.

The Balkan Wars

In 1912, Bulgaria, Serbia, Greece and Montenegro formed themselves into the Balkan League and attacked the Turks. By November, they had stripped the Ottoman Empire of nearly all its remaining European possessions. In 1913, Bulgaria attacked its fellow members in the League, but suffered losses that saw Serbia almost double in size. Austria-Hungary twice threatened Serbia with war if it did not withdraw from its new territories. But Serbia ignored the threats, and Austria-Hungary, lacking support from Germany or Italy, was forced to accept the fact of a larger Serbia to the south.

Some time before Archduke Franz Ferdinand's visit to Sarajevo, a plot had already been laid to assassinate him. As heir to the throne of Austria-Hungary he made an ideal target for the hatred that had built up among Serbs since Austria-Hungary annexed Bosnia six years before.

The man responsible for the plot was a Serbian army officer named Colonel Dragutin Dimitrijevic, otherwise known as Apis (the Bee). He was experienced in such matters, having organized the successful assassination in 1903 of the pro-Austrian King Alexander of Serbia. Apis had also sent a man to Vienna to kill Emperor Franz Joseph, and had plotted the assassination of Bosnia's governor, General Potiorek, in January 1914. But these two attempts had failed.

In 1911, Apis had founded a secret society called Union Or Death, better known as the Black Hand. The society was dedicated to the liberation of Serb peoples in foreign lands, and to the creation of a Greater Serbia. Its members included Serbian army officers, and the society exerted great influence over the Serbian government.

When he learned that the heir to the Austrian throne was due to visit Sarajevo in 1914, Apis began plotting an assassination. His chief aide, Major Voja Tankosic, set about recruiting the killers. In a coffee shop in Belgrade, the capital of Serbia, he enlisted three young Bosnian Serbs, all eager to strike a blow for Serbian liberation. Their names were Gavrilo Princip, Nedjelko Cabrinovic and Trifko Grabez.

Trifko Grabez, the son of a Serb priest. He was the only one of the seven assassins with a police record (for striking his high-school teacher).

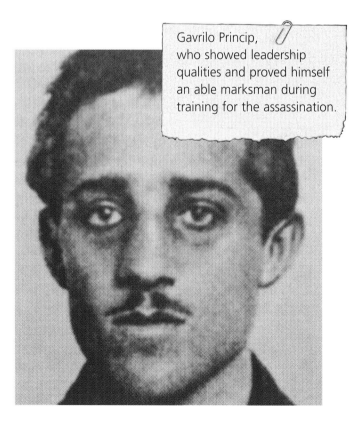

Gavrilo Princip, who showed leadership qualities and proved himself an able marksman during training for the assassination.

The three assassins were trained in bomb throwing and marksmanship, then smuggled back across the border to Bosnia on 3 June 1914. A fourth man, Danilo Ilic, joined the group and brought with him three more volunteers: Vaso Cubrilovic and Cvijetko Popovic, both seventeen-year-old students; and Muhamed Mehmedbasic, a Bosnian Muslim. They were recruited to make the group look more like a local gang than a team of Serb-organized terrorists. The seven assassins were supplied with four pistols and six bombs from Serbian army arsenals.

When word of the plot reached other leaders of the Black Hand and members of the Serbian government, they reacted with alarm. The assassination might spark a war between Austria-Hungary and Serbia, and the Serbians could not be certain that Russia would come to their aid. Apis was told not to proceed. He tried half-heartedly to stop the assassins at the border, but it was too late. Nothing more was done to stop Princip and his colleagues as they waited in Sarajevo for the arrival of the archduke.

Danilo Ilic, a former Sarajevo schoolteacher. He was a member of the Serb nationalist group Young Bosnia as well as the Black Hand.

The Torch

" A tiny clipping from a newspaper mailed without comment from a secret band of terrorists in Zagreb... to their comrades in Belgrade, was the torch which set the world afire with war in 1914. That bit of paper wrecked old, proud empires. It gave birth to new, free nations...The little clipping declared that the Austrian archduke Franz Ferdinand would visit Sarajevo, the capital of Bosnia, June 28 ... four letters and two numerals [June 28, which was Vid's Day] were sufficient to make us unanimous, without discussion, as to what we should do about it. "

Borijove Jevtic, a leader of National Defence – an organization linked to the Black Hand – describes the day news arrived of the archduke's planned visit.

In the 1900s, countries were often represented by their national symbols. This 1904 cartoon shows Russia (left) fighting Japan, watched by figures including Marianne (France), John Bull (Britain), the Kaiser (Germany) and Uncle Sam (USA).

WHAT WAS THE MOOD in Europe in the days and weeks leading up to the archduke's visit? The early summer of 1914, for those who lived to look back on it, was always recalled with nostalgia, as a time of innocence and happiness that was never to be repeated. It certainly promised to be an unusually good summer, with day after day of blue skies and sunshine. However, it would be wrong to suggest it was a time of perfect contentment. Every thinking person knew that the Great Powers were enjoying an uneasy peace.

Nationalism was at its height. In Britain, schoolboys were taught the Latin saying *Dulce et decorum est pro patria mori* – 'It is sweet and fitting to die for one's country'. Their country's national symbol was the muscular John Bull. In France the symbol of the nation was a mythical female figure named Marianne; in Russia it was the double-headed eagle; in Germany it was the German eagle and the Kaiser himself. Each country had a strong sense of its own identity, and an equally strong feeling of superiority over its rivals. This, along with fear of the intentions of the other powers, had led them into a frantic arms race.

The idea of a war in 1914 was highly appealing to many young men. They saw it as a pathway to glory, adventure and heroism. People were not generally aware in 1914 that advances in technology would mean a very different kind of war from the conflicts of the nineteenth century. There had been recent increases in the range and firepower of artillery, meaning that battlefields would become larger. The machine-gun, invented in 1862, had been developed into a fearsome weapon. In the hands of a defending army, it would make the spectacular cavalry charges of the previous century suicidal.

Unfortunately, the generals who should have been adapting their tactics to these new realities still held to traditional ideas of warfare. They failed to see that artillery, machine-guns and the recently developed barbed wire would give the advantage on the battlefield to the defence. They still believed that wars were won by the offensive and by getting their troops on the field faster than the enemy in order to gain the initiative.

In 1914, nearly everyone, from politicians to the ordinary public, had a romantic notion of war. The generals felt they were prepared. They had their huge armies, their mobilization schedules, their strategies and their rigid ideas of how the battle would be fought and won. In short, the world was ready for war.

Preparing for War

" We are witnessing this year increases of expenditure by the Continental Powers beyond all previous experience. The world is arming as it has never armed before. Every suggestion of arrest [stopping] or limitation has been brushed aside. "

Winston Churchill, January 1914.

Cannon in production at the Krupp factory in Essen, Germany, in 1914. Factories throughout Europe were trying to keep pace with the arms race of the Great Powers.

A 1910 photograph of Franz Ferdinand and Sophie with their children: (left to right) Ernst (six), Sophie (nine) and Maximilian (eight).

THE ASSASSINS LYING IN wait for Archduke Franz Ferdinand might have been surprised to know that he was not unsympathetic to their views. He understood the bitterness of the Slavs, and their desire for independence.

It was, in fact, the archduke's intention to one day offer the Slavs an equal voice in the government of the Austro-Hungarian empire. This idea made the archduke unpopular with the Hungarian nobility, who saw his plans as a threat to their power. It also brought him into conflict with his uncle, the emperor. It did not help that Franz Ferdinand was a proud man, who lacked the charm and social graces to make his arguments more persuasive.

The archduke was unpopular with the emperor and the court not only for his political views, but also for his choice of wife. Sophie Chotek had worked as a lady-in-waiting for Archduchess Isabella of Pressburg.

A Moment in Time

It is 5 June 1914, and Jovan Jovanovic, the Serbian Minister to Vienna, has a problem. His prime minister, Nikola Pasic, has asked him to warn the Austrian government of a plot to kill Franz Ferdinand in Sarajevo. But Jovan is not liked at the Austrian Foreign Ministry. He does, however, get along quite well with the Minister of Finance, Dr Leon von Bilinski. So, Jovan goes to Bilinski and tells him that, if the archduke goes to Sarajevo, 'Some young Serb might put a live rather than a blank cartridge in his gun and fire it.' Bilinski replies amiably: 'Let us hope nothing does happen.' Jovan has the feeling Bilinski has not understood, but this is the only effort he makes to deliver his vital message.

Nikola Pasic, prime minister of Serbia. His administration was marked by frequent disputes with the Serbian military and the Black Hand.

When Isabella had realized that Franz Ferdinand was visiting to see Sophie, rather than one of her eligible daughters, she had dismissed her immediately. The archduke declared his wish to make Sophie his wife, but Franz Joseph would not allow it. Although she had a title, she was regarded as too low-born to marry the heir to the throne of the Habsburgs. Only after Franz Ferdinand swore an oath giving up his future children's right to the throne, did the emperor consent to the match. On 1 July 1900, the wedding took place.

Sophie was never treated as a royal, and had to endure many public humiliations. For example, at formal events Sophie had to wait until all the higher-ranking women had made their entrances before she could join her husband. Yet the marriage was a happy one, and the royal couple were blessed with three children.

When, early in 1914, Franz Ferdinand received an invitation to visit Sarajevo, he did not think twice about accepting. Little did he realize the anxiety his planned trip would cause. In early June 1914, the Serbian prime minister, Nikola Pasic, learned of the plot to kill the archduke. If this succeeded, an investigation would reveal to Austria-Hungary the extent of the Serbian government's involvement with the Black Hand. Serbia would be blamed for the assassination, and this could lead to war. Yet, if Pasic warned the Austrians he would be seen as a traitor to his country. In the end, Pasic decided to issue a warning through diplomatic channels (see panel).

SUNDAY 28 JUNE 1914 was a warm and sunny day in Sarajevo. Crowds lined Appel Quay, the wide avenue that follows the north bank of the River Miljacka. They were waiting to cheer the royal couple. Many of the buildings on the avenue were decorated with flags and flowers.

10.00 am The royal party departed from the Philipovic army camp, where the archduke had inspected the troops. A motorcade, consisting of six cars, headed for City Hall for a reception hosted by the mayor of Sarajevo. Franz Ferdinand and Sophie were in the second car with Bosnia's governor, General Oskar Potiorek. The roof was folded down so the crowd could get a good view of the royal couple. A pennant bearing the Habsburg crest fluttered on the bonnet.

10.10 am As the procession moved along Appel Quay, the royal couple caught

A Moment in Time

The motorcade passes the first assassin, Muhamed Mehmedbasic. His nerve fails him and he does nothing. The second, Nedjelko Cabrinovic, is quicker to act. He takes the bomb concealed within his coat, strikes its firing cap against a lamp-post, and throws it directly at the archduke. He watches in disbelief as the bomb bounces off the car and explodes behind it. Cabrinovic is ill from tuberculosis – his life means little to him. He bites on a cyanide pill, rushes back through the crowd and leaps over a stone wall into the river. But the water is only a few centimetres deep, and the poison is so old it only makes him vomit. An angry mob drags the failed assassin from the river and he is handed over to the police.

their first sight of the crowds. There was little evidence of security, as the archduke had banned the army from the city streets for the day. He did not like the idea of a line of soldiers standing between himself and the people. It was left to the city's 120 policemen to ensure the archduke's safety.

Suddenly, as the procession approached the Cumurja Bridge, a black object flew out of the crowd. Franz Ferdinand saw what looked like a bomb hurtling towards him. He instinctively raised his arm to deflect it away from his wife, who was sitting to his right, closest to the danger. The bomb bounced off the folded car roof and into the street behind them. There was a loud explosion.

The driver, Franz Urban, accelerated to a safe distance then stopped. About a dozen spectators lay injured on the ground. The car behind had been hit with fragments of the bomb, and had stalled.

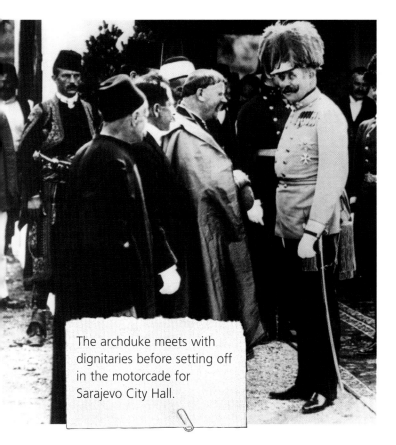

The archduke meets with dignitaries before setting off in the motorcade for Sarajevo City Hall.

Lieutenant-Colonel Eric von Merizzi, General Potiorek's chief adjutant, had received a bad cut to his head.

10.15 am The archduke ensured that the injured were taken to hospital, then the motorcade continued towards City Hall. Thinking about how unpopular he was at home, Franz Ferdinand commented bitterly that back in Vienna they would probably give the assassin a medal. He was unaware that there were other assassins still waiting in the crowd. Five of them watched as the motorcade sped past. It was now travelling too fast for them even to think about trying to assassinate the archduke.

Franz Ferdinand and Sophie are seated in the rear of the car as it sets off through Sarajevo. Count von Harrach, the car's owner, sits in the front with the driver Franz Urban.

DIAGRAM OF THE MOTORCADE
ROUTES AND POSITION OF ASSASSINS

FRANZ JOSEPH STREET

APPEL QUAY

MORITZ SCHILLER'S FOOD STORE

LATEINER BRIDGE

KAISER BRIDGE

RIVER MILJACKA

CUMURJA BRIDGE

KEY TO DIAGRAM

→ First journey: route to City Hall

▪▪▪▪▪▪▪▪▶ Original planned return route

━ ━ ━▶ Revised return route

Princip's shots

Cabrinovic's bomb

1 Muhamed Mehmedbasic
2 Nedjelko Cabrinovic
3 Vaso Cubrilovic
4 Cvijetko Popovic
5 Gavrilo Princip
6 Danilo Ilic
7 Trifko Grabez

21

City Hall as it looks today, where it is now the Sarajevo University Library.

The royal party arrives at City Hall after the bomb attack.

10.20 am At City Hall, the mayor of Sarajevo, Fehim Effendi Curcic, was faced by a furious Franz Ferdinand. The archduke shouted: 'Mr Mayor, one comes here for a visit and is received by bombs! It's outrageous!'

The mayor had ridden in the first car and was possibly unaware of what had just happened near Cumurja Bridge. Or perhaps he was mentally unable to deal with it. Whatever the reason, he simply launched into his prepared speech of welcome: 'Your Royal and Imperial Highness! Our hearts are full of happiness over the most gracious visit with which Your Highnesses are pleased to honour our capital city of Sarajevo, and I consider myself happy that Your Highnesses can read in our faces the feelings of our love and devotion, of our unshakeable loyalty, and of our obedience to His Majesty our emperor and king... '

After several minutes of this, Franz Ferdinand regained control of his temper. He replied: 'I thank you cordially for the resounding ovations with which the population received me and my wife, the more so

The archduke and his wife depart from City Hall, in the final moments of their lives.

since in them was heard an expression of pleasure over the failure of the assassination attempt.' Activities at City Hall then went ahead as planned.

A discussion was held regarding the rest of the archduke's schedule. Franz Ferdinand did not wish to cancel the original plans to visit the city's museum then have lunch at the governor's residence. But he did want to visit the hospital to check on Lieutenant-Colonel Merizzi and others injured by the bomb. A member of his staff, Baron Morsey, suggested that this might be dangerous. General Potiorek, who as Bosnia's governor was responsible for the safety of the royal couple, disagreed. 'Do you think Sarajevo is full of assassins?' he asked.

Potiorek turned to the archduke and said: 'Your Imperial Highness, you can travel quite happily. I take the responsibility.' He suggested that Sophie remain behind at City Hall, but she replied: 'As long as the archduke shows himself in public today I will not leave him.' Franz Ferdinand begged Sophie to do as the general suggested, but she would not hear of it.

A Moment in Time

With no certainty that the archduke will even pass their way again, the six remaining assassins have taken up new positions along Appel Quay. Gavrilo Princip is still among the crowd near Lateiner Bridge on the riverbank side of the avenue. But he is hungry, and he crosses Appel Quay to stroll down Franz Joseph Street. Princip reaches Moritz Schiller's food store, and steps inside to buy a sandwich.

11.10 am The motorcade set off once more. There were five people in the royal car: the driver Franz Urban, the archduke, Sophie, General Potiorek and the car's owner Count von Harrach. Potiorek thought it would be safer if they avoided the city centre, and he decided that the motorcade should travel all the way along Appel Quay to Sarajevo Hospital. Had he not been injured, the chief adjutant Merizzi would have passed this decision on to all the drivers. In the event, neither Franz Urban nor the mayor's driver in the leading car was informed of the change of route.

23

The driver of the mayor's leading car, still following his original directions, turned right off Appel Quay into Franz Joseph Street to head for the museum. When Franz Urban followed him, General Potiorek leaned forward and said: 'What is this? This is the wrong way! We're supposed to take the Appel Quay!' Urban applied the brakes, and the archduke's car came to a halt directly outside Moritz Schiller's food store.

Urban began to turn the car around, but the road was too narrow. So, he put the car in reverse. At that moment, Potiorek looked up to see a young man with hard eyes and a thin moustache step towards the car. The man aimed a pistol and two shots rang out. To Potiorek's ears, the report of the gun sounded unusually soft. He looked round at the royal couple seated next to him. They were sitting upright and seemed unharmed, so Potiorek assumed the shots had missed. The car pulled away, and he shouted at Urban to go directly to the governor's residence.

As the car sped across Lateiner Bridge, the archduke opened his mouth and a stream of blood spilled down his tunic. He had been shot in the neck, and the bullet

The blood-stained jacket of the archduke, worn on the day of his assassination.

An artist's impression of the assassination, which appeared in a French magazine, *Le Petit Journal*, a few weeks later.

A Moment in Time

Gavrilo Princip cannot believe his eyes when he sees the archduke's car slow down just three metres from where he is standing. He does not hesitate. Dropping his sandwich, Princip pulls a pistol from his pocket, steps up to the car's running-board and fires twice at point-blank range. Then he watches as the car speeds away. People are running towards him. Princip turns the gun on himself, but it is knocked away. He is in danger of being lynched by the angry crowd, but is rescued by the police. Before he is arrested, Princip swallows a cyanide capsule. But it is old, like Cabrinovic's. Princip is violently sick.

This photograph, taken in the confused moments just after the assassination, shows Princip (second from right) being arrested.

The archduke cried out: 'Sophie dear! Sophie dear! Don't die! Stay alive for our children!' Then he collapsed. Harrach seized him by the coat collar to prevent his head sinking forward, and asked him: 'Is Your Highness in great pain?' Weakly, Franz Ferdinand replied: 'It is nothing.' He repeated those words several times before losing consciousness.

11.30 am Both Sophie and Franz Ferdinand were unconscious when they arrived at Konak, the governor's residence. The staff doctor was hurriedly summoned. Minutes later, he informed General Potiorek that the duchess was dead. The archduke, he said, would not last more than half an hour. Potiorek, trying to keep his emotions under control, told an aide to prepare a message for Vienna. It would convey the significant news of Archduke Franz Ferdinand's death.

had pierced his jugular vein. As Count von Harrach took out his handkerchief to wipe away the blood, Sophie cried: 'For heaven's sake, what's happened to you?' She then sank down in her seat. Potiorek and Harrach thought she had fainted and tried to help her up. Then they saw blood on her, and realized that Sophie had been shot in the abdomen.

The trial of the assassins in October 1914. Seated in the front row, left to right, are Grabez, Cabrinovic, Princip and Ilic.

Gavrilo Princip (1894–1918)

Gavrilo Princip, the son of a postman, became interested in Serb nationalism while at school in Sarajevo. He travelled to Belgrade and joined the Black Hand at the age of eighteen, but had tuberculosis and was unfit for active duty. Two years later, Princip was recruited by Major Tankosic as one of Franz Ferdinand's assassins. After the assassination, Princip was jailed. He had an arm amputated because of tuberculosis of the bone, and died in April 1918 in a prison hospital. He became a national hero in Serbia. Moritz Schiller's food store is now the Princip Museum, and two footprints on the pavement outside mark where Princip stood to fire the shots.

AFTER THEIR ARRESTS, PRINCIP and Cabrinovic were interrogated by the Sarajevo police, who demanded to know who was behind the assassination. Both men remained silent about the role of Apis and the Black Hand, and insisted they had acted alone. Meanwhile, the other assassins fled the scene, hiding their bombs and guns. A few days later, Danilo Ilic was arrested by the Sarajevo police, who had discovered that Princip had stayed at his house.

Ilic lost his nerve. In the hope of avoiding the death penalty, he gave the police the names of everyone involved in the plot. His confession led to the swift arrests of Trifko Grabez and the two students, Vaso Cubrilovic and Cvijetko Popovic. By 5 July, the whole gang was in police custody with the exception of Muhamed Mehmedbasic, who had escaped south to the neighbouring country of Montenegro.

In October 1914, the six young Bosnian Serbs stood trial in Sarajevo's district court for the assassination. Ilic's confession had threatened to expose everything about the plot. But at the trial, the other five defendants followed Princip's lead in revealing nothing about the Black Hand. Princip stated: 'In trying to insinuate that someone else has instigated the assassination, one strays from the truth. The idea arose in our own minds, and we ourselves executed it. We have loved the people. I have nothing to say in my defence.'

A few of the assassins, though, expressed sorrow for what they had done. Cabrinovic said: 'Although Princip is playing the hero, and although we all wanted to appear as heroes, we still have profound regrets. In the first place, we did not know that the late Franz Ferdinand was a father. We were greatly touched by the words he addressed to his wife: "Sophie, stay alive for our children."'

The assassins were found guilty, but under Austrian law no one under twenty years of age could be sentenced to death. In Princip's case there was some doubt as to whether he was twenty or not. It was never established for certain whether his birthday had fallen a few days before or after he committed the crime. The court gave Princip the benefit of the doubt, and sentenced him to serve twenty years in prison.

Danilo Ilic was twenty-three years old. He had given the police the names of his colleagues in the hope that his life might be spared. Ironically, he was the only member of the gang sentenced to death. On 3 February 1915, Ilic was hanged.

Sophie and Maximilian, two of the murdered couple's children. At the trial, Princip offered apologies to the orphaned children for killing their mother, but said he was not sorry about killing the archduke.

Princip the Martyr

"There is no need to carry me to another prison. My life is already ebbing away. I suggest that you nail me to a cross and burn me alive. My flaming body will be a torch to light my people on their path to freedom."

Gavrilo Princip to the prison governor.

27

The funeral of Franz Ferdinand and Sophie in Vienna. Emperor Franz Joseph did not attend.

FOR A FEW DAYS after the assassination, Vienna was paralysed more with shock than with grief. Many of the Austrian and Hungarian nobility thought they were better off without the archduke and his ideas for sharing power with the Slavs. On hearing of his nephew's death, Emperor Franz Joseph was reported to have said: 'A higher power has re-established the order which I, alas, could not preserve.' He had regarded Franz Ferdinand's marriage outside the royal circle as a threat to the empire, and now he interpreted the assassination as a punishment from God.

The couple were not granted burial in Vienna's Capuchin Crypt, the traditional burial place of the Habsburgs. Instead, they were hastily buried in a crypt beneath the chapel of Franz Ferdinand's castle, Artstetten. Even in death, Sophie's social inferiority

was not forgotten. Her coffin was set lower in the crypt, and had far less decoration.

A wave of anti-Serb feeling swept through Austrian cities, and there were riots in Vienna. But the inquest into the assassination proved inconclusive. The only fact the investigation could establish was that the weapons had come from Serbia. The Austrian police commissioner, Friedrich von Wiesner, had been sent from Vienna to Sarajevo to take charge of the investigation. He reported: 'Nothing proves complicity of the Serbian government in carrying out the attack.'

This did not change the determination of some Austrian ministers to respond to the assassination by punishing Serbia. The aggressive Austrian Chief of Staff, Conrad von Hötzendorf, saw an opportunity to reduce the size of Serbia through war.

Count Stephen Tisza, the Hungarian premier, was opposed to the idea, as was Emperor Franz Joseph. Count Berchtold, the Austrian Foreign Minister, was undecided.

The argument was swayed by the reaction of Kaiser Wilhelm II of Germany. When he heard about the assassination, he responded: 'The Serbs must be disposed of, and that right soon!' Franz Joseph then wrote to the Kaiser asking for German support in case of war with Serbia. On 5 July 1914, Wilhelm informed his government that he had decided to offer Austria-Hungary full support, with a promise that Germany would come to the aid of Austria-Hungary if Russia attacked.

The following morning, the German chancellor, Theobald von Bethmann Hollweg, told the Austro-Hungarian ambassador that his government could count on German support whatever they decided to do. This became known as the 'blank cheque', because it gave Austria-Hungary complete licence: the actions and policies of Germany, Europe's strongest power, would now be decided by Austria-Hungary's war-hungry government. Shortly after this, the Kaiser went off on his yacht for a three-week summer cruise.

Kaiser Wilhelm II (1859–1941)

The eldest grandchild of Queen Victoria grew up to be a vain, insecure man of unstable temperament. He had a love of war, and a powerful sense of his own importance. He did nothing to prevent Europe slipping into war in 1914, and encouraged the process with his 'blank cheque'. During the war, his popularity declined. With his uncompromising attitude, he came to be seen as an obstacle to peace. After Germany's defeat in 1918, he fled to the Netherlands where he lived the life of a country gentleman until his death in 1941.

Wilhelm II (left) and Franz Joseph on a postcard from 1914. The Kaiser's offer of unconditional support for the Austro-Hungarian emperor greatly increased the chances of war.

EVEN AFTER RECEIVING THE German offer of support, the Austro-Hungarian ministers continued to argue over how they should deal with Serbia. Finally, on 14 July 1914, they reached a decision. The government would send an ultimatum to Serbia which was so severe that it was bound to be rejected. They would then be able to blame Serbia for starting any conflict.

The sending of the ultimatum was delayed when it was realized that the army was not ready – important units were on leave, many of them on their farms gathering the harvest! The ultimatum was finally sent on 23 July. It demanded that Serbia ban all anti-Austrian newspapers and organizations within its country;

remove all anti-Austrian individuals from the military and civil services; and allow Austria-Hungary to conduct an investigation on Serbian soil into the assassination. Acceptance of these demands would have reduced the Serbian government virtually to the status of a puppet regime of the Austro-Hungarian Empire.

On 24 July, the rest of Europe realized how serious the crisis had become. The Russians were determined not to back down in the face of Austro-Hungarian aggression as they had when Austria-Hungary annexed Bosnia in 1908. Tsar Nicholas II, Russia's ruler, ordered his troops to mobilize, in case of an Austrian attack on Serbia. Russia offered Serbia its support, but called for caution.

The Ultimatum

" The history of the past few years, and particularly the painful events of the 28th of June, have proved the existence of a subversive movement in Serbia, whose object it is to separate certain portions of its territory from the Austro-Hungarian Monarchy… The Serbian government has done nothing to suppress this movement. It has tolerated the criminal activities… directed against the Monarchy… and it has tolerated, finally, every manifestation which could betray the people of Serbia into hatred of the Monarchy and contempt for its institutions. "

From the Austro-Hungarian ultimatum to Serbia, 23 July 1914.

In the summer of 1914, mobilization posters like this one from France appeared in towns and cities throughout Europe.

The mobilization of German forces is announced in Berlin on 31 July.

Kaiser Wilhelm II and Tsar Nicholas II (saluting) in 1913. In an exchange of telegrams at the end of July 1914, the two leaders blamed each other for the descent into war.

The Serbians listened to this advice. They replied to the ultimatum on 25 July, accepting all of the Austro-Hungarian demands except one – they refused to grant Austro-Hungarian officials the right to conduct an investigation on Serbian territory. Realizing that this might provide enough of an excuse for Austria-Hungary to attack, the Serbian government ordered the mobilization of its army even before the reply had been delivered.

On receiving the reply, Austria-Hungary broke off diplomatic relations with Serbia, and mobilized half the imperial army. On the same day, France assured Russia of its support in the event of a war with Austria-Hungary. The terrible chain reaction that the alliance system had always threatened was now set in motion.

On 26 July, Britain proposed a conference to resolve the crisis. France and Russia both agreed, but Austria-

Hungary refused to gamble its national prestige on the outcome of an international debate. Germany supported its ally in this decision. But on 28 July, the Kaiser began to have second thoughts. He said that, with the Serbian reply to the Austrian ultimatum, 'Every reason for war disappears.'

The Kaiser's change of heart came too late. On the same day, Austria-Hungary declared war on Serbia.

In Munich, cheering crowds greet the news that war has been declared. Among them, caught by chance in this photograph, is Adolf Hitler, the future dictator of Germany.

DURING THE LAST DAYS of July and the first days of August 1914, Europe slipped towards war. The politicians and diplomats could not keep pace, and the generals took control of events. This was inevitable, since the military plans of the Great Powers depended on the following of strict timetables. Once the war machines of Europe had been set in motion, they were almost impossible to stop.

Austria-Hungary was the first nation to declare war. The Austro-Hungarian leaders wanted a war with Serbia, and had feared that the opportunity might slip away if peace talks took place. But the Austro-Hungarian army could not be fully mobilized until 12 August.

Although its army was not yet ready to fight, on 29 July Austria-Hungary began shelling Serbia's capital, Belgrade. On hearing news of this, the German government became divided. The Chief of Staff, Moltke, wanted to mobilize his troops. But the Kaiser and the chancellor, Bethmann Hollweg, still hoped for peace. They urged the Austro-Hungarian government to talk again with the Russians.

In the Russian capital of St Petersburg, Tsar Nicholas could not make up his mind whether or not to mobilize the army. On 30 July, he finally gave the order. On 1 August 1914, Germany declared war on Russia. War in Eastern Europe was now inevitable. The interlocking alliance system made its spread to

Western Europe likely, but not yet certain. Blame for that must lie with the German war plans. Because of the Franco-Russian Alliance, Germany had potential enemies to the east and west. So, in the 1890s General Alfred von Schlieffen had devised a plan for Germany to fight both France and Russia (see panel). This entire military strategy depended on attacking France first. Now that war with Russia had broken out in the east, the Germans' strategy left them no choice but to attack France in the west.

On 2 August, in accordance with the Schlieffen Plan, Germany invaded Luxembourg. The next day, the Germans declared war on France and invaded Belgium. On 4 August, Britain – which was committed to supporting Belgium and France – declared war on Germany. On 6 August 1914, Austria-Hungary declared war on Russia. The Great Powers were all now in the conflict. Germany and Austria-Hungary on one side were lined up against Russia, France and Britain on the other. The First World War had begun.

The Schlieffen Plan

Germany's war strategy, the Schlieffen Plan, was based on the belief that the Russians, because they did not have a decent railway system, would take six weeks to mobilize. In this time, the German army would mount a decisive, two-pronged attack against France. The left wing of the German army would defend the border with France, while a powerful right wing swept through Belgium to encircle the French forces. Schlieffen had estimated they would achieve victory in precisely six weeks. Having defeated France, the German army would then transfer to the east to fight the Russians. In August 1914, the Schlieffen Plan was set in motion.

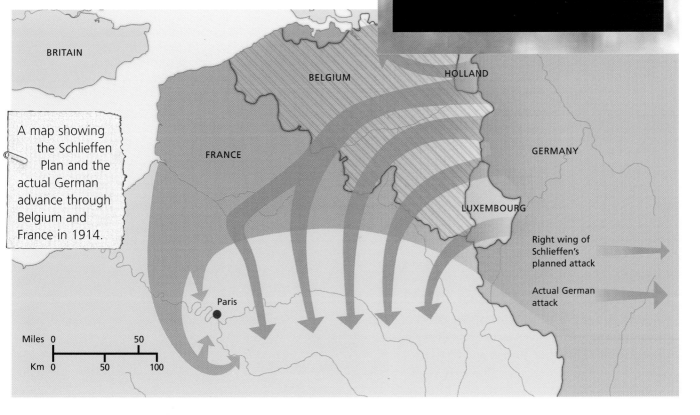

A map showing the Schlieffen Plan and the actual German advance through Belgium and France in 1914.

BRITAIN

BELGIUM

HOLLAND

FRANCE

GERMANY

LUXEMBOURG

Right wing of Schlieffen's planned attack

Actual German attack

Paris

Miles 0   50

Km 0   50   100

THE OUTBREAK OF WAR was greeted with confidence and jubilation by most people in Europe. Few imagined how long or disastrous the conflict would turn out to be. It was common to hear people say that their troops would be 'home by Christmas'.

On 14 August 1914, the French attacked the Germans in Alsace and Lorraine – territories they had lost in the Franco-Prussian War of 1871. The attacks failed, and the French suffered appalling casualties. It quickly became clear that lines of troops charging with bayonets could not advance against machine-guns. Meanwhile, the Germans had put the Schlieffen Plan into action. Their right wing had advanced through Luxembourg, then swiftly crushed the Belgians. The Allies (the British and French) now tried to halt this advance, but they were simply overpowered.

A Force of Nature

" What came after [the advance party], and twenty-four hours later is still coming, is not men marching, but a force of nature like a tidal wave, an avalanche or a river flooding its banks... At the sight of the first few regiments of the enemy we were thrilled with interest. After they had passed for three hours in one unbroken, steel-gray column we were bored. But when hour after hour passed and there was no halt, no breathing time, no open spaces in the ranks, the thing became uncanny, inhuman. You returned to watch it, fascinated. It held the mystery and menace of fog rolling toward you across the sea. "

An American, Richard Harding Davis, observes the German army entering Brussels.

By the start of September, the Allies had retreated south almost to Paris. But Moltke had made changes to his strategy, and there were fewer troops in the advancing right wing than Schlieffen had suggested. Now, fearing a Russian attack, Moltke took even more troops away and sent them east. As the German right wing became weakened, the Allies made a stand at the River Marne, about 120 km from Paris. Between 5 and 10 September, they halted the onslaught and forced the Germans into retreat. The Schlieffen Plan had failed. France was undefeated, and the Russians were mobilized. The Germans now faced what they had feared most – a war on two fronts.

The Allied and German armies were now concentrated in eastern France, north of Paris. Between late September and November, they fought a series of bloody battles. Each side tried to advance around the other's flank, in a desperate struggle towards the ports on the English Channel which provided vital supply lines between France and Britain. This became known as the 'Race to the Sea'.

Neither side won the race, and the losses each suffered were appalling. At Ypres, in Belgium, the British 7th Division went into battle with 12,300 troops and

emerged with just 2,400 alive. With the onset of winter, the front along which the Allied and German armies faced each other gradually became more settled. The exhausted troops of both sides now began to dig trenches for protection from enemy fire.

By the end of the year, a continuous, 765-kilometre line of trenches stretched from the French coast to the Swiss border. The Western Front had been established.

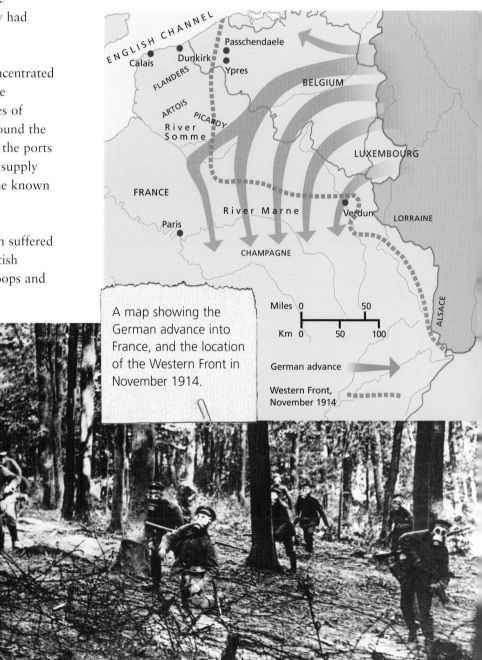

A map showing the German advance into France, and the location of the Western Front in November 1914.

German troops wearing gas masks advance through woods during the Battle of the Marne.

A British soldier in a flooded trench in France, 1917. The harsh living conditions left troops vulnerable to terrible illnesses.

IN MAY 1915, THE French attacked the German lines at Artois. The battle lasted a month and cost 150,000 French casualties, without achieving any breakthrough. The German defensive system of trenches and strongholds was too strong, and the French artillery too weak. The military leaders of the Great Powers had predicted a war of movement. But this was not possible when attacking such well-defended positions. The defending army – with its trench systems supplied by rail with men, weapons and ammunition – could always reinforce itself more quickly than the advancing army. The result was a grim deadlock.

For ordinary soldiers, life in the trenches was incredibly tough. Keeping clean was almost impossible. Lice infested soldiers' clothing, and in winter trenches became waterlogged. Soldiers lacked a decent diet, and many became ill.

Between the opposing lines of trenches lay 'no-man's land', a devastated wilderness of mud and shell-craters. In 1916, the generals on both sides tried to break the deadlock by launching major offensives across this area. These attacks were usually preceded by a prolonged shelling of the enemy, designed to weaken and demoralize them. Thousands of troops were then ordered to go 'over the top' and charge across no-man's land towards the enemy trenches.

In February, a German offensive at Verdun was met with determined defence by the French. Appalling casualties were suffered by both sides, for no significant gain. In July, the British launched an offensive at the Somme. German machine-guns and artillery cut down wave after wave of attackers, and there were 60,000 British casualties on the first day alone. By November, the British had managed to advance just ten kilometres.

In 1917, new weapons began to appear. Grenades and mortars were used to attack machine-gun posts. Tanks were used by the Allies, but they proved unreliable and a breakthrough still proved impossible. It was another year of horrendous casualties and little territorial gain.

By early 1918, the effects of huge losses and a war on two fronts had seriously weakened the German army. An offensive launched in the spring of 1918 foundered, and by summer large numbers of American troops were arriving in France. The USA had initially been neutral, but had declared war on Germany in April 1917 after American ships were attacked by German submarines. In October, the Germans decided they had no option but to agree an armistice.

First World War graves at Passchendaele cemetery in Belgium. The vast majority of casualties were young men. Among German men aged 19 to 22 when the war began, the death rate was one in three.

First World War Military Losses

The number of soldiers killed in the First World War has been estimated at about 10 million, the wounded at about 20 million.

COUNTRY	DEAD	WOUNDED	PRISONER
Russia	1,700,000	4,950,000	2,500,000
France	1,385,000	3,044,000	446,000
Britain	947,000	2,122,000	192,000
Italy	460,000	947,000	530,000
USA	115,000	206,000	4,500
Serbia	45,000	133,148	152,958
Germany	1,808,000	4,247,000	618,000
Austria-Hungary	1,200,000	3,620,000	2,200,000
Turkey	325,000	400,000	250,000
Bulgaria	87,500	152,390	27,029

William L. Langer, Encyclopaedia of World History (Houghton Mifflin, 1972).

AUSTRIA-HUNGARY HAD GONE to war in 1914 to punish Serbia for the assassination of Archduke Franz Ferdinand. In doing so, it had hoped to reduce the smaller country's power to create mischief in the future.

This French cartoon uses Franz Joseph to represent Austria-Hungary's humbled status in 1918. The shadow of the Kaiser suggests how Germany had contributed to its ally's downfall.

However, with the involvement of Germany and Russia, Austria-Hungary's own war aims were quickly forgotten. Germany used the opportunity instead to unleash an attack on its powerful rivals in Europe. Austria-Hungary was no longer able to focus its efforts solely on defeating Serbia. Instead, under the terms of its alliance with Germany, it was obliged to protect the Germans' eastern front against Russia.

Repeatedly in 1914 and 1915, Austria-Hungary was forced to call upon Germany for military help. This was necessary firstly to reinforce its faltering armies against the Russians at Galicia, in the Ukraine. Later, Austria-Hungary needed help to protect its southern front against Italy, which joined the war on the Allied side in May 1915. Austria-Hungary did defeat Serbia's small but determined army in November 1915, but only with the help of German and Bulgarian forces.

By the end of 1915, Austria-Hungary was weary of war. There had been little cause for joy in Vienna. It was clear that the armies were struggling, and any victories they had achieved were due largely to German help. The defeat of Serbia had also done nothing to solve the problem of the empire's discontented minorities.

In November 1916, Emperor Franz Joseph died. He left the declining empire in the hands of his inexperienced grand-nephew, Charles. Even in the midst of war, Charles found the Austrian parliament constantly divided between the various nationalities of the empire. The process of war, far from uniting the empire, only hastened its collapse. In October 1918, the Austro-Hungarian armies began to fall apart under a sustained assault by the Italians. There were mutinies by national minorities, as well as surrenders and desertions.

Charles tried to open secret negotiations with the Allies, in the hope of taking Austria-Hungary out of the war. But he found that the Habsburg monarchy was no longer seen as a legitimate government. The Allies, especially the USA, were sympathetic to the national independence movements of the Bosnian Serbs and others. The Austro-Hungarian Empire finally collapsed in October and November 1918 when Hungary, Czechoslovakia, Croatia and German-Austria declared independence and formed separate countries.

Bosnia joined a newly created state for southern Slavs, called the Kingdom of Serbs, Croats and Slovenes. It also included Serbia, Montenegro, Herzegovina and other Slav territories formerly belonging to the Austro–Hungarian Empire. In 1929, it would be renamed Yugoslavia.

Charles I (1887–1922)

Charles was born in Persenberg, Austria, the nephew of the murdered Archduke Franz Ferdinand. In 1916, he proclaimed himself Charles I, Emperor of Austria-Hungary, and Charles IV, King of Hungary. His attempts to deal with discontented minorities by granting them equal powers in government could not prevent the empire's collapse on 3 November 1918. Charles abdicated nine days later. In 1921, he made two unsuccessful attempts to regain the Hungarian throne, before being deported to the island of Madeira.

Charles I (centre), the short-lived emperor of Austria-Hungary. Here, he inspects his troops in Galicia.

Princip (right) and Cabrinovic (left) in June 1914 with Milan Ciganovic, who instructed them in the use of guns and bombs. The success of their carefully planned operation in the end relied on a large degree of luck.

LET US IMAGINE THAT Gavrilo Princip had not crossed Appel Quay to buy a sandwich at Moritz Schiller's food store on that June day in 1914, to find himself by chance in shooting range of the archduke's motor car. How different might history have been if Franz Ferdinand and Sophie had not been assassinated in Sarajevo, and had continued with their visit before returning safely to Vienna?

According to most historians, we would probably still be living in a world that experienced a major war in that period. The summer of 1914 might have come and gone peacefully, but sooner or later a conflict between the major powers would probably have occurred. As early as December 1912, many German leaders had accepted that war was inevitable. From their statements at the time, it appears that Kaiser Wilhelm II and Helmuth von Moltke actually wanted

a war. The Germans were surrounded by hostile powers, and they believed the only way to survive was to attack first. In Austria-Hungary, war was seen as a way of uniting the empire. Assassination in Sarajevo was not the cause of war, but an excuse for it.

There had been several crises between 1905 and 1913 that might have led to war. Yet, the Great Powers pulled back from the brink each time. Austria-Hungary's annexation of Bosnia in 1908 did not lead to war because Russia was too weak to support Serbia at the time. The 1912–13 Balkan Wars did not trigger a wider conflict because the Great Powers were not directly involved, and only Austria-Hungary was unhappy with the outcome. Why was the Sarajevo crisis in 1914 different? Because not only did Austria-Hungary want war, but Germany was willing to support its ally. And Russia, this time, was not prepared to back down.

The earlier crises had increased tensions between the Great Powers. And it certainly seems, in hindsight, that a war of some kind was bound to break out. Yet, one recent historian, Graham Darby, in *Origins of the First World War*, warns us against such an assumption: 'We should always be aware that nothing is inevitable in history... and that last-minute changes in events can lead to a completely different outcome. Perhaps the First World War would not have happened if Archduke Franz Ferdinand's driver had not taken a wrong turning in Sarajevo.'

Out of control

" The great majority of the peoples are in themselves peaceful, but things are out of control and the stone has started to roll... "

Theobald von Bethmann Hollweg, chancellor of Germany, 30 July 1914.

" I foresee that very soon I shall be overwhelmed by the pressure forced upon me and be forced to take extreme measures which will lead to war. "

Tsar Nicholas II, in a telegram to the Kaiser, 29 July 1914.

" The responsibility for the disaster which is now threatening the whole civilized world will not be laid at my door. In this moment it still lies in your power to avert it. "

Kaiser Wilhelm II, in a telegram to the Tsar, 31 July 1914.

Footprints have been made to mark the spot where, by chance, Princip was standing when he shot the archduke and his wife.

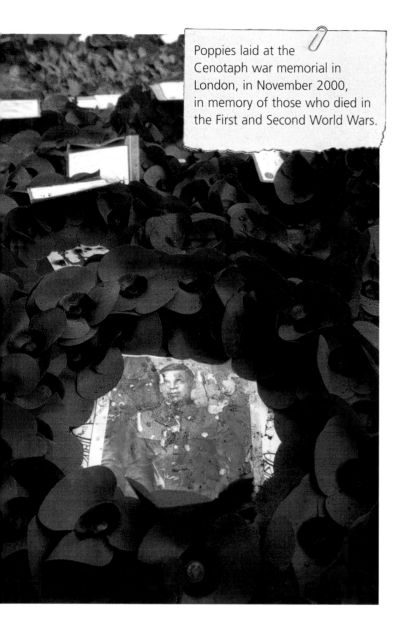

Poppies laid at the Cenotaph war memorial in London, in November 2000, in memory of those who died in the First and Second World Wars.

CLEARLY THE MOST IMPORTANT legacy of the assassination in Sarajevo was the First World War. It was the first truly global conflict, and the scars remain to this day. It hastened the collapse of the Austro-Hungarian Empire, and led to the birth of several new nations. These included a new southern Slav nation, Yugoslavia. So, in the end, the assassination achieved its aim.

The Serbian desire to be a major force in the Balkans continued to burn throughout the rest of the twentieth century. Serb nationalism was suppressed by the communist regime which ruled Yugoslavia after 1945. But it re-emerged with the collapse of this regime in the 1980s. Since 1945, Yugoslavia had contained six separate republics, each with its own republican government, yet all bound together under a central communist government. This system began to fall apart in 1990 when Slobodan Milosevic took control of the republican government in Serbia.

On 28 June 1989 – Vid's Day, the 600th anniversary of the Battle of Kosovo, and the anniversary of Franz Ferdinand's assassination – Milosevic made a speech announcing his intention to reshape Yugoslavia.

Milosevic's regime called for the creation of a Greater Serbia, uniting all Serbs in a single state. This idea horrified the other republican governments of Yugoslavia; and Slovenia, Croatia and Bosnia declared their independence. Both Croatia and Bosnia had large Serb populations, and Serbia would not tolerate their decision to leave Yugoslavia. A Yugoslav army led by Serbs attacked Croatia in 1991, beginning a four-year conflict. In April 1992, the Serbs attacked Bosnia, laying siege to the city where Franz Ferdinand had been shot, Sarajevo.

The war continued until November 1995, when a peace agreement was signed under pressure from NATO (the North Atlantic Treaty Organization, a military alliance of the Western powers). Serb nationalism did not disappear, however. In the 1990s, Serbs began driving non-Serb minorities out of Kosovo, a small province with strong historical links to Serbia. Major conflict broke out again in 1998, and was only resolved after NATO air-strikes.

Milosevic fell from power in 2001, and was eventually handed over to the International Criminal Tribunal at The Hague to stand trial for war crimes. But the forces he represents have not gone away. They are currently contained by international pressure, but the underlying problem has not been solved. Just as in 1914, the Balkans remains a region in which nationalism can easily erupt into conflict.

A girl from Kosovo holds pictures of her brothers and sisters. They were killed by Serb forces in March 1999, during their brutal campaign to drive out non-Serb minorities.

What Happened to the Other Assassins?

- Apis was arrested in 1917, in a government crackdown on the Black Hand. He was sentenced to death for treason, and shot at sunrise on 24 June 1917.

- Nedjelko Cabrinovic was sentenced to twenty years in prison. He died in January 1916 of tuberculosis.

- Vaso Cubrilovic received a sixteeen-year prison sentence. Released in 1918, he became Minister of Forests for Yugoslavia.

- Trifko Grabez admitted his guilt, and was sentenced to twenty years. He died in February 1916 of tuberculosis.

- Muhamed Mehmedbasic was implicated, along with Apis, in a new assassination plot. He was imprisoned, then pardoned in 1919. He returned to Sarajevo to work as a gardener and carpenter.

- Cvijetko Popovic received a thirteen-year sentence. He later became curator at the Sarajevo Museum.

Glossary

abdicate Give up a high office, especially the throne.

adjutant A military officer who assists a commanding officer and acts a little like a secretary.

air-strikes The dropping of bombs and missiles by aircraft.

alliance A formal association between nations, especially for purposes of defence.

annexation The absorbing, or taking over, of a territory by another country.

armistice A truce in war to discuss terms for peace.

arms race A race between countries to build up their armed forces and armaments.

arsenal A stockpile of weapons and military equipment, or a building where they are stored.

artillery Large guns.

Austro-Hungarian Empire The Austro-Hungarian Empire, or Austria-Hungary, was a large and powerful country at the centre of Europe between 1867 and 1918 (see panel on page 8).

bayonets Sharp, dagger-like weapons attached to the ends of rifles.

cavalry The part of an army made up of soldiers on horseback.

centenary The celebration of one hundred years.

Chief of Staff The senior officer serving on a military staff, responsible for managing it and advising the commander.

communist regime A government in which a single party controls the means of production, with the aim of establishing a classless society.

confederation An alliance of small states.

cross-examined Questioned closely in court.

crypt A room under a church where the coffins of the dead are placed.

cyanide A type of poison.

diplomacy The work of dealing, and making agreements, with other countries.

Entente A French word meaning an international agreement. It is an understanding rather than a formal alliance.

ethnic group A group of a certain race, or a group that shares the same customs, language and culture.

firing cap A mechanism that ignites an explosive charge.

flank The side of a body of troops.

front An area where armies are facing each other, or fighting between armies is taking place.

imperial Concerning or involving an empire.

inquest An official inquiry to find out how a person died.

jugular vein Any one of four pairs of veins in the neck that drain blood from the head.

manoeuvres Troop movements conducted on a large scale, usually as a rehearsal or practice for war.

marksmanship Skill and accuracy in firing guns.

mobilization The assembling and preparation of troops for war.

mortar A cannon used for firing shells at a high angle over a short distance.

motorcade A procession of cars or other vehicles, especially forming an escort for someone important.

mutiny A rebellion against legal authority, especially by soldiers or sailors refusing to obey orders and often attacking their officers.

nationalism Loyalty and devotion to a nation. Sometimes, also a belief that a nation is better than other nations and has the right to dominate them.

offensive An attack or assault.

Ottoman Empire The empire of the Ottoman tribes, a Turkish Muslim people. It lasted from about 1300 to 1922, and at its height included lands in Turkey, northern Africa, south-western Asia and parts of south-eastern Europe including the Balkans.

propaganda Publicity intended to make people believe something.

province An administrative region or division of a country.

puppet regime The government of a country whose actions and policies are controlled by another, more powerful, country.

report A sharp, loud noise, especially that of an explosion or gunshot.

republican government The regional government of a republic, which is also part of a national government.

running-board A flat ledge on which it is possible to stand, which runs beneath the bottom of the doors on some old cars.

subversive Disloyal, taking part in activities aimed at undermining a government.

terrorists People who use violence in order to achieve political goals.

treaty An agreement between different countries, for example setting out the divisions of land after a war.

tuberculosis A serious disease that affects the lungs.

ultimatum A final demand from one country to another, which, if it is not met within a stated time, will lead to war being declared.

Further Information

Reading

Armistice 1918 by Reg Grant
(Hodder Wayland, 2000)

Assassination in Sarajevo by Stewart Ross
(Heinemann, 2001)

The Frightful First World War by Terry Deary
(Scholastic, 1998)

The War in Former Yugoslavia by Nathaniel Harris
(Hodder Wayland, 1997)

The War in the Trenches by Ole Steen Hansen
(Hodder Wayland, 2000)

What They Don't Tell You About World War I
by Bob Fowke (Hodder Children's Books, 2001)

Sources

Origins of the First World War by Gordon Martel
(Longman, 1996)

Origins of the First World War by Graham Darby
(Longman, 1998)

The Establishment of the Balkan National States, 1804–1920 by Charles and Barbara Jelavich
(University of Washington Press, 1986)

The Long Fuse: An Interpretation of the Origins of World War I by Laurence Lafore
(Waveland Press, 1997)

The Origins of World War I by Joachim Remak
(Thomson Learning, 1995)

Websites

www.ibiscom.com/duke
This site has eyewitness accounts of the assassination.

www.spartacus.schoolnet.co.uk/FWW.htm
An encyclopaedia of the First World War.

www.iwm.org.uk
Britain's Imperial War Museum.

www.geocities.com/CapitolHill/6777/sarajevo
A history of Sarajevo.

Timeline

1871 Prussian victory in the Franco-Prussian War leads to a united Germany.

1873 The Three Emperors' League is formed between Germany, Russia and Austria-Hungary.

1878 The Treaty of Berlin grants Austria-Hungary control of Bosnia.

1879 Germany signs the Dual Alliance with Austria.

1882 The Dual Alliance becomes the Triple Alliance when Italy joins.

1894 France makes Russia its ally.

1900 Archduke Franz Ferdinand marries Sophie Chotek.

1907 Britain joins France and Russia to form the Triple Entente.

1908 Austria-Hungary annexes Bosnia.

1911 The Black Hand is founded.

1912–13 The Balkan Wars: Bulgaria, Serbia, Greece and Montenegro attack Turkey; then Bulgaria attacks Serbia, Greece and Montenegro.

3 June 1914 The assassins are smuggled across the border from Serbia to Bosnia.

5 June 1914 The Austro-Hungarian government is given a veiled warning about the plot to assassinate the archduke.

28 June 1914 Archduke Franz Ferdinand and his wife Sophie, Duchess of Hohenberg, are assassinated by the Bosnian Serb Gavrilo Princip, in Sarajevo, Bosnia.

6 July 1914 Germany offers its support to Austria-Hungary in whatever action it decides to take against Serbia.

23 July 1914 The Austro-Hungarians send an ultimatum to Serbia.

25 July 1914 The Serbians reply to the Austro-Hungarian ultimatum, refusing to concede only one point.

28 July 1914 Austria-Hungary declares war on Serbia.

1-3 August 1914 Germany declares war on Russia and France, and invades Luxembourg and Belgium.

4 August 1914 Britain declares war on Germany.

6 August 1914 Austria-Hungary declares war on Russia.

October 1914 The six Bosnian Serbs involved in the assassination are tried and found guilty.

August–November 1914 Three attacks by Austria-Hungary are repulsed by Serbia.

November 1915 Austro-Hungarian, German and Bulgarian forces defeat and occupy Serbia.

November 1916 Emperor Franz Joseph dies, and is succeeded by his grand-nephew Charles I.

April 1917 The USA joins the war on the side of the Allies.

3 November 1918 The Austro-Hungarian Empire collapses.

11 November 1918 An armistice is signed between Germany and the Allies, bringing the First World War to an end.

12 November 1918 Charles I of Austria abdicates.

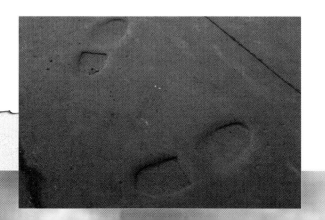

Footprints mark the spot where Princip's shots shook the world.